A PLACE APART
THE CAPE BRETON STORY

TEXT BY JAMES B. LAMB
PHOTOGRAPHS BY WARREN GORDON

LANCELOT PRESS
HANTSPORT, NOVA SCOTIA

Published 1988
Second printing 1992 by
LANCELOT PRESS LIMITED
Hantsport, Nova Scotia
Office and production facilities located on Hwy. 1,
1/2 mile east of Hantsport, N.S. B0P 1P0

ISBN 0-88999-379-3
Printed in Hong Kong

Production co-ordinated by
Stone House Publishing Inc.,
P.O. Box 9301, Station A, Halifax, N.S.
B3K 5N5

ACKNOWLEDGEMENT
This book has been published with the assistance of
The Nova Scotia Department of Tourism and Culture.

Front cover photo: *Aspy Bay*
Back cover photo: *Glace Bay Harbour*

CONTENTS

THE ISLAND

Most visitors see it first as it appears from the mainland shore of Nova Scotia, a long series of receding headlands, rising abruptly from the sea, backed by wooded uplands and wrapped in a blue haze; enormous, mysterious, beautiful. Bathed in sunshine or glowering under storm cloud Cape Breton is never just another pretty island; seeming immense and impenetrable, despite the Canso causeway bridging its moat, it is, as it has always been, a world apart, a place, a people, a way of life like no other.

Cape Breton, in a sense, is a distillation of Nova Scotia; here the flavour of the province is stronger, with more bite and tang. Where Nova Scotia — 'New Scotland' — is Scottish, Cape Breton is Highland Scots; where Nova Scotia is lovely, Cape Breton is beautiful; where Nova Scotia has charm, Cape Breton is breathtaking.

Although linked by a causeway to the mainland since the 1950s, Cape Breton is still very much an island, a place apart, and the sense of a separate identity is still fiercely cherished by the people who live here, and who trace their island roots back over innumerable generations. It is an identity still evident in a distinctive speech and culture, and manifested to the visitor in an old-world hospitality and sense of values that have long disappeared elsewhere. Notoriously independent and politically perverse, they are proud to be 'Caybretoners' but are tolerant of the foibles of mere mainlanders and to tourists 'from away' they extend the traditional Gaelic 'Caid Mille Failte'; 'One hundred thousand welcomes.'

Physically, the island is beautiful as well as diverse; magnificent beaches alternate with awesome cliffs towering above the sea; great mountains, wrapped in dense forest, overlook peaceful pasturelands bordering placid pools and streams; grim coal mines are only a stone's-throw from lovely countryside. It is a place apart, visually stunning, and its distant hills, veiled in their distinctive blue haze in both sunshine and shadow, impart an intriguing sense of enchantment to this island world.

Cape Breton; a place apart.

At the base of Cape Smoky

BEGINNINGS

On a lonely, windswept beach, a stone figure stares with sightless eyes out over the empty waters of Aspy Bay. Here, on these level sands stretching away into the distance on either side, and in the looming shadow of magnificent Sugarloaf Mountain, John Cabot is thought to have made his landfall on his voyage of discovery to the New World, and to have landed to replenish his water casks from the turbulent Wilkie Brook, which here tumbles into the sea. His bust stands atop its stone plinth as the centrepiece of a little provincial park near the northern tip of Cape Breton Island, a memorial to the courage and enterprise of the early European navigators, and the scenic road that encircles the northern headlands now bears his name.

But Cabot was by no means the first European to reach these island shores. The Vikings, from their Newfoundland base at Lance aux Meadows, explored these waters in the Dark Ages, and described the island in their sagas. Fishermen from the Breton coast of France gave their name to the island, and the Portuguese built a fort, which they called Nigonish, to protect their fishdrying frames on the sands of what is now called Ingonish Beach. Fishermen from Spain harvested cod from the Spanish Banks off the approaches to Sydney harbour, and fishing vessels from Cornwall and north Devon regularly watered at the island before setting out on the long return passage home with their heavy catches of cod.

But the experiences of these illiterate fishermen survive only as an oral tradition; it remained for the first official voyages of exploration, sent out from Europe to establish the boundaries of a great New World, to put Cape Breton officially on the map. Jacques Cartier sighted Cape North enroute to the Gulf of St. Lawrence and to his ascent of that river that led to the founding of New France, but it was not till later that Cape Breton was established, by some nameless navigator, as an island separated from the continental mainland.

From the earliest times, Cape Breton has been the site of European settlement, from the transient fishermen, huddled in huts about their catches drying in the sun on a waveswept beach, to the first planned settlements of the French and the Scots in the opening years of the 17th century. With abundant wood and water, excellent natural harbours and ideal location on the shortest great circle routes from Europe, the island boasts some of the earliest European settlement in Canada.

But these settlers, however enterprising, were merely intruders into a land with a long-established native Indian population. Excavations on Ingonish Island and elsewhere reveal that organized native communities existed here centuries before the birth of Christ.

FORTS

The early history of Cape Breton island was written in blood, and has left as its legacy an abundance of ancient fortifications; no other part of Canada can boast so many forts in so small an area. They were built by the earliest European arrivals — Portuguese, French, Scots, British, Americans — as protection against one another, and, in the beginning, also against the native Indians.

Today, Cape Breton's forts constitute one of the island's main attractions for visitors. The mighty fortress of Louisbourg is Nova Scotia's single biggest tourist site, and has been restored to its 18th century glory, but the grassgrown ruins of the smaller, older forts add romance to the rugged landscape for the discerning visitor who takes the time to look for them. Most of them are completely undeveloped, mere mounded earthworks marked, perhaps, with an inscribed cairn at best, their secrets hidden beneath the ground awaiting the excavator's spade, and they range from primitive stockaded earthworks surrounding some 17th century settlement, to the sophisticated concrete batteries which protected Sydney harbour in World War Two.

The outline of Fort Dauphin is visible on the lawn next to the Englishtown ferry slip.

Oldest, and most intriguing of all, is Fort Dauphin, built by the French in 1629 at the narrow entrance to St. Ann's Bay, near Englishtown. Sited to command the approaches to the Gulf of St. Lawrence and the river which was quickly recognized to be the key to Canada, the little fort became the springboard for both Champlain's explorations and the Jesuit missions to the Indians of New France. In Englishtown today, a confused jumble of mounds and bumps and a cairn mark the site of this early fort, and the graves of the 48 French soldiers, including the victim of the first European duel fought in the New World, who died there.

In 1713 a new fort was built which for six busy years was the principal French base, before the tendency of the harbour to become choked with ice prompted a move to Louisbourg.

Other forgotten forts include the site of Fort Rosemount at Baleine, near Louisbourg, built by Lord Ochiltree in 1629 as the first Scots settlement in the New World but captured by the French in the same year; Nicholas Denys' trading fort at the entrance to the modern canal at St. Peters, and the later British fort, still well preserved, on the heights above, both now maintained within a pleasant park. A small garrison of British regulars was based here as late as the 19th century, to guard this strategically vital entrance to the Bras d'Or Lakes.

The latest fortifications on the island were the artillery forts built to command the approaches to Sydney Harbour, a principal convoy assembly port and one of the world's power centres in World War Two.

LOUISBOURG

Louisbourg, the great fortress built in the 18th century as the principal French base and defence for New France, is absolutely unique. Nothing like it exists anywhere else in the world, and it remains the largest single fortification ever constructed in the New World by a European power.

From its very beginning in 1719 everything about the new base was on a colossal scale. The cost of its construction was so staggering that the French monarch is said to have jokingly looked out his palace window at Versailles to see whether he could glimpse its towers rising above the western horizon. It was more than a fortress; it was a town and a trade centre and a fishing port and a naval base, all sheltered within a complex of defence works patterned on the concepts of Vauban, the French fortification genius. Its harbour, while not so large as the St. Ann's base which it replaced, could shelter the largest navy, and its busy dockyard provided the stores and artisans necessary to maintain a New France fleet. Although plagued by fog and rain much of the year, its harbour was relatively ice free the year around, and its location athwart the Quebec trade route, near the fishing banks and menacingly close to rival British interests in Boston and New England, gave France the initiative in its desperate struggle for New World supremacy.

Alas for French hopes; Louisbourg, designed by a Paris bureaucracy remote from the site, had two fatal flaws. The first was a matter of topography; it was vulnerable to assault from the rear, where rising ground overlooked its walls, and the other was psychological; much of its strength was dependent on a complex of detached outworks, whose garrisons, when under attack, tended to escape to the safety of the stronger citadel and abandon their defences to the enemy. Both these weaknesses were soon evident; Louisbourg was assaulted only twice, and both times fell to attackers who landed in the rear and used the guns of abandoned French batteries on the harbour shore and island to bombard the central fortress. A combined New England and Royal Navy Force captured Louisbourg with relative ease and a few years later the fortress, restored to the French by treaty, was taken again by British regulars under General Wolfe, enroute to the capture of Quebec and the ending of New France in 1759.

Totally destroyed, the great French stronghold has been miraculously restored today in all its 18th century blend of glitter and squalor, so that the visitor may marvel at the gilded splendour of its lovely salons and the crowded discomfort of its barracks. Life goes on within the town today much as it did more than two centuries before; uniformed regiments march, costumed townspeople go about their daily tasks.

Louisbourg is THE Nova Scotia tourist site; an absolute must for any Cape Breton visitor.

THE FRENCH

French roots in Cape Breton are long and strong; for a time in the 18th century when the rest of the Maritimes had been ceded to the British, the island remained a French enclave as Isle Royale. But when Louisbourg fell for the second time, all the French who could afford the passage — officers, merchants, officials, landowners — returned to France with their families. The people who remained, peasants and fishermen, gravitated over the years into two areas, centred on Isle Madame at the southern extremity and Cheticamp on the northwest coast.

Today, both areas still retain their distinctive Gallic flavour. The 'French Coast,' as it is called, can be traced on a map by its French placenames, extending from Belle Cote to Cap Rouge, and Cheticamp at its centre is a French fishing town, pure and simple, clustered about its beautiful cathedral-like church. On Isle Madame the tiny communities, each with its French name, cling tenaciously to their rocky islet rising from a turbulent sea, and in both places French remains the vital language of the people along with the universal English of the marketplace.

But French influence has left its mark in other parts of Cape Breton. In the days of imperial glory, the enormous official establishment at Louisbourg was sustained by food grown on Boularderie Island, the long, fertile piece of land set apart by the ocean inlets at the Great and the Little Bras d'Or. Named for the Sieur de Boularderie, a distinguished French nobleman and soldier who settled it with peasants brought out for the purpose from France, the island was intensively farmed in the distinctive New France manner and became the breadbox of the French army, and a source of timber for the growing town and dockyard at Louisbourg. Today Boularderie still retains its uniquely French field patterns, each narrow property, walled off from its neighbour, running down to the water which once provided its access to the outside world. Here, too, Man o'War point marks the site of a shipyard where a French frigate was burnt on the ways by the victorious British.

French handicrafts and music are a major part of Cape Breton's cultural heritage, and are much enjoyed by visitors to the island, especially along the French shore, but the community here is not the Acadia of some romantic poet's imagination, recreated for tourist purposes in the 20th century. There is none of that mainland nonsense here; French, Scots, Irish or Polish, these are all 'Caybretoners,' and proud of it.

Petit de Grat

THE SCOTS

More than anyone else, it is the Scots who have imparted Cape Breton's distinctive flavour; tough, dour, God-fearing Highlanders from the barren coasts and islands of northwest Scotland, they arrived here early in the 19th century, driven from their ancestral homes by the breakup of the communal clan system and the harsh economic pressures that gave sheep priority over people. They settled here, much as they had at home, in family units, separated according to religion and place of origin, Lewis folk here, Barra people there, Harris families next door; this side of the water Presbyterians, the other side 'the men of Rome,' as Catholics were known.

To this day, the same regional divisions remain in place, so that Iona, with its great church and hill dominating the lovely Barra strait, is still a centre of the Roman Catholic faith lapped about by a Presbyterian sea, and any Cape Bretoner can place another islander by the mention of his name.

This concentration of clan families, all with a common surname, has led to the use of nicknames to differentiate between one person in an area and another. MacDonalds and MacLeods are so thick on the ground, for example, that they are frequently distinguished by physical characteristics; Big Roddy perhaps, or Black Billy or Red Rory. Descendants could then be similarly distinguished — Big John's son Kenneth being known as Kenny Big John. Often it was a man's trade that was reflected in his nickname; a well-known Baddeck firechief, surnamed MacDonald, lived and died as Kenny Sparks, and even simple geography could determine a nickname, so that in one clan settlement a man who lived at the top of the hill was known all his life as Johnny Up, while his neighbour at the foot of the hill was, of course, Johnny Down.

Accustomed for generations to making the most of very little, taciturn and austere, these hardy people carved out of the forbidding rock and forest of their new home a vibrant community that reflected much of the way of life they had left behind in the Western Isles and Highlands, and the names they gave their new communities breathe of their Scottish origins; Inverness and Dingwall, New Glasgow and Piper's Cove, Barrahead and Hector Point.

The kind of life they lived is preserved today in the Highland Village, on the heights above Iona. Here the houses, barns, mills and shops of pioneer days have been sensitively restored, and the visitor can step back into a way of life that has long vanished. Yet even in the hectic 20th century world of television and automobiles, something of the old ways still linger in Cape Breton in the strong sense of community, of clan pride and family feeling and, above all, in a sense of values beyond the merely material concerns that so bedevil people 'from away.'

Ferry crossing from Iona to Grand Narrows

THE GAELIC

It is a curious coincidence that St. Ann's, the lovely bay on Cape Breton's eastern shore that was the site of the island's earliest French settlement, should also have been the location chosen by the first of the Scots settlers whose descendants today give the island its distinctive Highland flavour. Here, in 1819, the Reverend Norman MacLeod arrived with several shiploads of followers, and established a tight-knit community which survived, through every adversity, to establish a truly Scottish Cape Breton. A religious fanatic but a man of great strength of intellect and character, Norman MacLeod ruled his little kingdom with an iron hand before famine and economic failure forced a move, in 1851, to more promising conditions in New Zealand. Although in his 70s, the indomitable MacLeod inspired his little flock to build a ship, the *Margaret*, on the shores of their bay, and to sail in it to the other side of the world, leaving behind the very young and the old, and a tradition of Scots hardihood which still characterizes the island.

The ruins of MacLeod's house, and those of his flock; of their church and mill and shipyard, lie in the overgrown fields and orchards along the northern shore of the bay's 'South Gut,' but their true memorial is to be found on the hillside above. Here, an impressive assembly of buildings standing in beautiful grounds house The Gaelic College, a unique institution devoted to the perpetuation and promulgation of Gaelic language, music and culture, and attended by students from all parts of North America.

This remarkable school is the creation of a remarkable man, a sort of 20th century reincarnation of Norman MacLeod named Angus W.R. MacKenzie, universally known simply as 'A.W.R.' A Highland Scottish Presbyterian minister like his forerunner and equally imbued with crusading fervor, A.W.R. arrived at St. Ann's after service with the Black Watch in World War One, and was dismayed at the rapid disappearance of traditional Scottish values under the onslaught of the automobile, the radio and the all-pervasive American culture they brought to Cape Breton. A man of single-minded purpose, great eloquence and tireless determination, this penniless preacher single-handedly organized a little band of dedicated workers and raised the funds, at the height of the Great Depression, to purchase the old Norman MacLeod colony property. Here they built the dormitories and classrooms of the world's first Gaelic College, and organized the classes in piping, Scottish dancing and Gaelic language which helped revive the island's flagging heritage and spread Scottish culture to every corner of the continent.

Here, on the shores of lovely St. Ann's Bay, this modern college and the overgrown ruins of the original Scots colony embody the Highland heart of Cape Breton.

Highland dancers from Gaelic college, St. Ann's Bay

THE MARGAREE

One of the world's most famous salmon streams, the Margaree River, has made Cape Breton a special place for fly fishermen everywhere. Its two branches, the Southwest and the Northeast Margaree, rise many miles apart in the rugged, mountainous interior, and drain vast areas of wooded upland before meeting at Margaree Forks to run in majestic splendour to the sea at Margaree Harbour on Cape Breton's western shore.

There are salmon to be found in many other island rivers and streams, of course, and even in some of Cape Breton's ocean estuaries, but it is the Margaree that is the centrepiece and showplace of the Cape Breton sports fishing industry, drawing fishermen to it from all over the world. There are little camps and cabins and hotels, scattered along its shores catering to the accommodation of these sportsmen, and at Northeast Margaree there is even a salmon fishing museum, illustrating every aspect of the famous river fishery, from rods and tackle used over the years to some of its most celebrated catches.

Yet there is a great deal more to the river than mere fish and fishermen. The river, especially its lower sections where it combines the waters of both branches, has scoured out over the ages a broad, deep valley, and it is here, in the fertile fields of river silt and the green water meadows, that some of the island's loveliest rural scenery is to be found. In vivid contrast to the mountainous background, the river, here broad and slow-moving, winds its way through a peaceful valley of unsurpassed beauty, with cattle grazing in the lush meadows on either side. This is magnificent farming country, and broadwalled barns and gabled farmhouses add color and variety to the prevailing greenery.

The valley is dotted with tiny villages, each boasting Margaree in its name, for all are proud of their river heritage; Upper and Lower, East and West, Beach and Harbour, Centre and Forks, there is a Margaree of some sort to suit everyone. Each painted white, with contrasting trim, the houses cluster about their clapboard churches and crowded graveyards, for these are old communities in a long-settled area whose fertile, well-watered fields have been an attraction since the arrival of the first farmers.

Here, in the magnificent mountain wilderness of the New World, generations of hardy men and women have fashioned a beautiful countryside and a distinctive way of life, that reflects the aspect and values of the Old World, a sheltered valley whose restful tranquility is all the more appealing for the magnificent mountain wilderness beyond.

Salmon fishing on the Margaree River

THE BRAS d'OR

Cape Breton Island is shaped like a hollow tooth, with an outer shell of land enclosing a watery centre. The Bras d'Or Lakes, as this hollow centre is called, are salt water, open to the sea from three outlets, at St. Peter's canal, a man-made cutting at its southwestern tip, and through the Great and Little Bras d'Or channels on either side of Boularderie Island, both natural openings to the Atlantic on the eastern shore of Cape Breton. Because the salt ocean water is supplemented by a considerable inflow of fresh water from several rivers and innumerable brooks, the levels in the lake vary considerably from those of the sea outside, so that while the two eastern entries are at sea level, that at St. Peters requires a lock, with a fall of several feet, varying according to weather conditions, to the ocean outside. Tides within the lake system are quite unpredictable, changing with barometric pressure and rainfall, but in any event levels vary little, the tidal range being a matter of inches rather than feet.

Depths within the system reach a thousand feet in one channel, and there are few shoals or reefs, but the entire system is dotted with islands, mostly uninhabited and wooded. This great complex of open water, sheltered from ocean wind and wave, and with channels in every direction leading to magnificent scenery and unspoiled beaches and islands, make the Bras d'Or Lakes an unsurpassed attraction for sailing and boating enthusiasts, and indeed knowledgeable yachtsmen have rated it as the world's greatest unspoiled cruising ground. Large yachts from the eastern seaboard of the United States, together with others from the Great Lakes and eastern Canadian ports plus a considerable fleet of locally based pleasure craft cruise here each summer, yet the complex is so large and the bays and coves so many and secluded that a yacht might cruise all day without sighting another vessel, unless its owner chooses to take part in one of the regular large sailing regattas.

The yachting centre of the Bras d'Or is at Baddeck, whose picturesque and sheltered harbour provides both a large and active yacht club and a complete range of facilities for chartering, servicing, supplying, repairing and storing yachts of every size. Baddeck, too, is home to one of Canada's most famous yachts, the venerable yawl *Elsie*, built for Alexander Graham Bell's family and the flagship of the Cruising Club of America, which regularly cruises to the Bras d'Or to do honor to the lovely yacht in whose saloon the club was founded. And at the top of Baddeck Bay a world-famous globetrotter, the celebrated brigantine *Yankee*, lies on the bottom in her final resting place, her wanderings ended and still visited by admiring yachtsmen from many parts of the world she once knew.

The Elsie passing Baddeck lighthouse

FISHERMEN

It was medieval fishermen, drawn by the incredible abundance of northern cod on the teeming Grand Banks and Gulf of St. Lawrence, who first settled on Cape Breton, and for more than 500 years the fishery has been a dominant theme of island life. The origins of some of the tiny fishing villages, especially along the eastern shore, are lost in the mists of time, but men have been leaving them to work the fishing grounds since before the beginnings of recorded Cape Breton history, just as they continue to do today.

Fishing, and the toil, discomfort and danger of plying the trade on the stormy North Atlantic, winter and summer, have left an indelible mark on the character of both the island and its people. To the visitor, the little clusters of white-painted houses, huddled about the spindly wharves of a sheltered harbour on the rocky, waveswept coastline, are the very essence of Cape Breton scenery, and such picturesque ports as Main-a-Dieu or Petit-de-Grat, Ingonish or Neil's Harbour are among the most photogenic of the tourist's island circuit. But to the native Cape Bretoner, fishing is often a way of life and its fortunes play a vital part in the island economy. More than coal or sheep or steel or timber, fishing is what Cape Breton is all about, and poor catches still mean hard times in island towns.

But fishing has changed enormously over the past few decades. Cod, while still a staple, is no longer the sole catch; new, more sophisticated markets have opened up for crab, groundfish and, of course, that gourmet staple, the Atlantic lobster.

But it is new technology which has most revolutionized the Cape Breton fishery. Sonar has made fish-finding more exact, radar has removed much of the danger of fog and darkness, loran and satellites have made position-finding precise and easy, and radio has established a vital link between ship and shore. Today's fleets setting out from island harbours represent investments of many millions of dollars, and their technology is both expensive and ever-changing. Dingwall and Cheticamp, Glace Bay and St. Ann's, these and dozens more like them are vital Cape Breton industrial centres as well as picturesque beauty spots.

Most of the hundreds of fishing craft registered on the island are engaged in the inshore fishery, setting out to fish by the day or overnight before returning with their catches, but the larger ports are home to a new breed of boat, the big steel-hulled stern trawlers who work far offshore, and are away for a week or more. Their huge catches, along with those of their more numerous and smaller sisters, are cleaned and packed in the big barn-like processing plants which are a feature of Cape Breton fishing ports, and breathe life into island stores and businesses, for fishing is the lifeblood of the island.

Fishing off Wreck Cove

WILDLIFE

Cape Breton is more like a miniature continent than a mere island; within its confines are mountains and inland seas, pastoral uplands and dense forests, rural valleys and immense stretches of sun-drenched sand. Two-thirds of its area is occupied by a massive central spine of mountain, heavily wooded and the source of innumerable rivers and streams, and with a distinctive climate quite different from that prevailing in the lowlands and coastal areas below. These are the famous Cape Breton Highlands, and more than anything else they give the island its distinctive appearance and provide much of its scenic splendour.

Vast areas of these forested fastnesses have never been trod by man; lumbering roads and rough paths traverse some of the lower slopes, but much of the remoter hilltops are virtually inaccessible, and provide refuges for birds and animals in numbers and variety that have long disappeared from mainland Nova Scotia. Black bear and the ubiquitous white-tailed deer are common, and moose are now to be found throughout the highlands area. The bald eagle is found in Cape Breton in numbers unmatched anywhere on the eastern half of the continent, feeding on the fish that throng both the rivers and the Bras d'Or lakes, as does

the osprey, that magnificent fish hawk, and the stately great blue heron. Fox are found everywhere in the island, but are especially numerous in the highlands, while the lynx and bobcat, shy and rarely seen by man, still flourish in the spruce forests of the uplands. Coyotes, or brush wolves, have recently appeared on Cape Breton, and rumours persist of sightings of the occasional mountain lion, or cougar.

Perhaps no predator is thicker on the ground, however, than the wily raccoon, that masked and merry bandit whose rowdy families are such a tumultuous part of woodland life, and whose curiosity and penchant for getting into mischief are so exasperating to people living in rural areas.

But there are some surprising gaps in the range of wildlife on the island. The visitor is struck by the absence of skunks and porcupines, both abundant on the mainland and such noticeable casualties along summer highways. For some reason not yet known, although the island has been linked to the mainland by a causeway for more than thirty years, neither animal has yet ventured to cross on the relatively short span of highway or railway over the Canso Strait, let alone swim the cold salt water, as so many other animals have done ages before.

Yet it can surely only be a matter of time before these two notorious wanderers manage to cross safely, and join the great array of wildlife which make up one of Cape Breton's most appealing attractions.

Mary Ann Falls

THE CABOT TRAIL

Of all the many and varied attractions of Cape Breton, probably none is better known, or has greater appeal, than the Cabot Trail. More than anything else, it is this spectacular scenic drive, no more than 128 miles in all, that draws visitors to the island, arriving not only individually in automobiles, caravans and campers but by the bus-load and cruiseship-load. The Cabot Trail is famous all over the world, one of Canada's premier tourist attractions, and yet for all its hyperbole it is something that has to be experienced and savoured individually, for it is not the same thing to everyone.

To begin with, there is endless debate as to whether it is best to make its circuit clockwise or counterclockwise; those advocating the first point out the advantages of always being on the inner part of the steep mountain circuits, giving the driver more time to enjoy the scenery and having the western sun behind for the afternoon run, while those who prefer the other, more traditional route get better views of the magnificent western coastline stretching ahead as they descend. Whatever the choice the scenery is both varied and spectacular, and not to be missed on any account.

Traditionally, the route begins and ends at Baddeck, and the circuit is broken roughly into several distinct parts, each with its own character. The run up the Margaree Valley is a joy in itself, the lovely river valley, with its lush farmlands and sleepy villages being one of the island's premier beauty spots. The river mouth, with its vistas of sand and fishing shacks, can be a wildly exciting place in a western gale, while the brightly-painted berry-box houses of the French shore and the busy shops of Cheticamp have a uniquely Gallic tang and charm and are famous for their wide range of regional handcrafts. But it is the breathtaking beauty of the mountainous Cape Breton Highland National Park that is the most memorable part of the route; a circuit that climbs high above the sea, with views along the coast in both directions, then crosses a cloud-high plateau before descending along an equally spectacular east coast, through picturesque villages, and then the final ascent and descent of Cape Smoky and the rugged coastal run past Ingonish, with its gorgeous beaches, and the shimmering silver of St. Ann's Bay.

There are innumerable beauty spots enroute. Each visitor will leave with his own favorite memory, and there are special delights for the discerning driver who ventures a mile or two off the regular route; the poignancy of the Lone Shieling, perhaps, or the sunlit peace of the aptly named Pleasant Bay; formidable Money Point; Dingwall and Neil's Harbour and their fishing fleets, the sands of Aspy Bay and the lonely monument under Sugarloaf Mountain to John Cabot, who gave his name to this unique Cape Breton trail.

ALEXANDER GRAHAM BELL

More than a hundred years ago Alexander Graham Bell, weary from his exertions in developing his latest invention, the telephone, sailed up the Great Bras d'Or to Baddeck in the course of a holiday cruise. Captivated by the charm of the little village and the beauty of its setting, he decided to stop over for a few days. He is there still.

Enervated by the summer heat of his Washington home, Bell was enchanted by the clear fresh air and cool, refreshing nights of Cape Breton, and resolved to make it his summer home. In the end, of course, it became a much closer attachment than that; Baddeck became the true spiritual home of this great genius, his link with his faraway Scottish birthplace and the place where he felt most truly relaxed and at peace with himself, his mind, free from its wearisome Washington fetters, eager to explore whatever caught its fancy.

The fruits of those explorations, the creations of one of the world's greatest inventive geniuses, are to be found today in one of Canada's most celebrated museums, assembled in a striking architectural complex that is itself unique. Set on a hillside at the eastern end of the village, the Bell Museum looks out over Baddeck Bay towards Beinn Breagh, the 'Beautiful Mountain' where the great inventor lived for so many years and where he, together with his beloved wife Gertrude, lies buried in lonely splendour, looking out from the mountaintop over the waters of the Bras d'Or he loved so well.

In this fascinating collection is the battered fuselage of the HD4, the huge hydrofoil which established a world water speed record in this very bay, together with a full-scale replica of this marvellous machine. There are kites, rocket-propelled boats, the first iron lung, the earliest air screw propeller, and, above all, a variety of the world's first pioneer flying machines, all either in the original or in model or photographic reproductions, together with such diverse items as experiments in sheep breeding and fresh water distillation. A separate building nearby houses a full-scale replica of the Silver Dart, designed and flown by J.A.T. McCurdy, one of the bright young men in Bell's Aereo Experimental Association, and flown off the ice of Baddeck Bay in the first manned flight in the British Empire.

Bell's descendants still live in his magnificent Scottish baronial home overlooking the lakes above Red Head, his restless spirit still roams the wooded hillsides and memories linger of the days when men first soared aloft here in huge kites and spindly flying machines, or came roaring down the bay amid sheets of spray, great gouts of flame and a noise like thunder.

CHURCHES

Churches — churches — churches! Churches big, and churches small; churches with spires, churches with towers; Roman Catholic churches, Anglican churches, United churches, Presbyterian churches, Pentecostal churches, chapels of free thinkers; they are all here in Cape Breton, and in amazing numbers, so that the visitor is left with the impression that islanders are obsessively religious.

Certainly religion has played a dominant role in the settlement patterns and social organization of the island, and today, as always, religious feelings run strong. The schism within the Presbyterian and Methodist churches in the earlier part of the century awoke strong feelings, often splitting families as well as congregations, and it is not unusual to see two large churches standing actually side by side in a tiny hamlet, and representing a new congregation's attempt to upstage its former parent church.

Cape Breton churches are invariably well looked after; however remote the village, however small the congregation or insignificant the church, the building is always well maintained and kept immaculate, inside and out, and freshly painted. Generally, they are constructed of wood on a frame and clapboard design;

the number of churches built of stone or brick can be counted on one hand. This reflects the prevailing abundance of both wood and carpenters on the island, brick and masons being correspondingly scarce. Most smaller churches were designed on simple lines by the men who would later worship within it; plain men, able to turn their hand to almost anything, and whose churches still speak to us of the strong faith of a strong people. Invariably, the church is the dominant building in every Cape Breton community, reflecting the belief that in a Christian community God's house must be given priority over merely mortal concerns.

While simple rectangular buildings, with added tower and spire, are such a feature of all Cape Breton scenery, there are many buildings of exceptional beauty. Sometimes this stems from their design; the great churches of North Sydney and Sydney Mines, built by ship's carpenters and executing in wood Old World features intended for stone. Sometimes it is due to location; Arichat's church clinging to its rock above the sea, Mabou's towers dreaming above a placid river, Whycocomagh's spires facing one another across its lovely bay.

Some churches impress by their magnificence, like Cheticamp's cathedral-like building; others by their simplicity, some tiny saltbox, perhaps, set beside a barren shore. But large or small, it is Cape Breton's churches that add a unique character to any island view, and represent man's noblest ornament to its lovely landscape.

FARMING

They line every rural backroad, stand at a respectful distance beside every highway; some gaunt and neglected but most still cheerful with paint and hard use. They are Cape Breton farmhouses and they speak to every passerby of the people who built them there and of the life they led, long ago.

Small and plain and sturdy, standing four-square to the elements in little fields hewn out of the native bush, they reflect the character of the dour Highland Scots who built them and raised their families there and wrung a meagre living from their stony fields and pastures. For the first island settlers agriculture meant bare subsistence farming and, truth to tell, nothing much has changed since; Cape Breton farming is still largely a matter of a few cows, pigs and chickens, with an acre or two of a cash crop and orchard and garden to supply the family fruits and vegetables, with perhaps a horse in the barn for old times sake.

Here and there, in the lush river valleys and the occasional fertile patch in the interior, there are farms to match the rich acres of the mainland, and in recent years the rolling hillside grasslands of the southwest coast have become successful sheepfarming country, but generally speaking the island soil is too thin to support the large-scale crop and stock production and factory farming methods that mark 20th century agriculture elsewhere.

Yet for all that, farming has always been a way of life for many islanders and a house on the land, eked out with full or part-time work in a nearby town, is still a familiar Cape Breton pattern.

And in many ways, it is an eminently satisfying one, providing a full and varied daily routine together with strong ties to the family home and the land it stands on. No one accumulates great wealth, but then no one needs to starve, and in any event there is still a tendency among Cape Bretoners to regard any rich man — a fellow with more than five thousand dollars put by, say — as, if not perhaps really dishonest, at least not above suspicion.

The island's little farmhouses speak eloquently of the character, not only of the people who built them, but of those who live there now; old and weary and weatherworn, perhaps, like the aging couple inside, or bright and neat and cheerful like the lively family whose children tumble about outside. Here and there, a windowless wreck, almost hidden by the encroaching bushland, speaks of defeat; of death in the family, perhaps, or plain failure, but more often farmhouses here breathe a more cheerful air, for island roots to the land are deep and tough.

Farm near Mabou

SYDNEY HARBOUR

The occasional cruise ship and the ferries from Newfoundland supply some animation to the lower wharves, but the upper reaches of Sydney Harbour today are tranquil and empty, apart from a handful of yachts nodding at their moorings. There is little here to remind the visitor that this was once one of the world's busiest ports, and an Allied power centre in World War Two.

For five years Sydney was a convoy assembly point for shipping from the entire eastern seaboard of North America, which was then shepherded through U-boat wolf packs across the North Atlantic to wartorn Britain and Europe. Its immense harbour was once crowded with scores of merchant ships, and its naval dockyard thronged with the warships of the escort groups which were to protect them on their perilous passage. Sydney was the sailing port of the notorious SC convoys; notorious because the slow speed of the elderly ships comprising most convoys from the port made them a prime target of Nazi submarines. The climactic battles of the war at sea were fought around SC convoys, which thus witnessed both the costliest failures and the most resounding successes of the Battle of the Atlantic.

There is little now to remind the visitor of Sydney harbour's days of greatness. Empty waters mark the former anchorages of rows of rust-streaked merchantmen, and the wartime unloading berth on the city of Sydney side is today Government Wharf, used by visiting cruise ships. The naval dockyard at Point Edward, across the harbour, is now an industrial park, and its wharves are home to ferries and other vessels under repair or laid up. Big ships still sail from the jetties of North Sydney, but they go no further than Argentia or Port aux Basques on their regular ferry crossings. A few concrete ruins, neglected and weedgrown, mark the gun emplacements and observation towers of the artillery forts that once protected the wartime port, but they are the last tangible reminders of Sydney's finest hour, when its magnificent harbour, the island's largest and North America's easternmost, was a place of world significance.

The harbour is still an interesting place to visit, offering spectacular vistas across its wide stretches of sheltered water. Shorebirds and small craft add a deceptive rural intimacy to its narrow westerly anchorages, but blustery winds and the salty tang of the sea at its wide-open entrance mark this for what it still is; an inlet of the North Atlantic and one of Canada's finest natural harbours. The run along its northern shore offers the visitor the best views of Sydney's skyline as well as an interesting mixture of sea, sky and scenery.

Sunrise, Sydney Harbour

COAL MINING

When the first French settlers arrived in Cape Breton early in the 17th century, they found coal lying in lumps, along the shoreline in various parts of Cape Breton. This surface coal was used to supplement the wood fuel, cut from the surrounding forest, to heat their homes, but more importantly it was used, from earliest times, in the blacksmith and gunsmith forges that were so vital to an iron-hungry settlement.

But it was not until the 18th century, and the development of Louisbourg as a great military and naval base, with thousands of people concentrated in a relatively small area, that island coal began to be intensively mined. The major coal finds along the eastern shore date from this time, although only few were developed, but from its beginning the big French base, with its booming dockyard and forges and hundreds of individual hearths, both military and domestic, was self-sustaining for fuel.

The industry lapsed with the fall of Louisbourg, and little was done to develop island mines for a hundred years. But the coming of the age of steam, and the resultant industrial revolution in Victorian England, had a dramatic impact on fuel use throughout the world, and nowhere more than in Cape Breton.

Commercial mines were developed all about the Sydney Bay area, and soon gave rise to a whole collection of mining villages and towns, including Sydney itself, Sydney Mines, New Waterford, Glace Bay, Dominion and, over on the western shore, Inverness. Coal mining became a way of life and although many of the mines were eventually worked out, some after tunnelling far out under the sea bottom, or became uneconomic to operate for one reason or another, coal mining has left a deep mark on the island and its people.

To the visitor the mining towns of Cape Breton are one of the island's most distinctive sights. Apart from the stark towers at the shafts themselves, it is the orderly rows of small, frame houses, square in plan and elevation and often set uncomprisingly in the middle of barren rock or on the very lip of the sea, that are a Cape Breton hallmark. But it is the miners and their families, hardened by years of exposure to the dangers, difficulties and discomforts of a miner's life with its 'boom and bust' cycle, that add so much to the island's distinctive character, and make Cape Breton islanders a very special kind of people.

Visitors can now experience something of the underground life by visiting a special Miner's Museum in the area, or take a trip down the shaft of an abandoned mine now set aside for their use. And a famous choral group of local miners, The Men of the Deep, bring traditional Cape Breton songs and harmony to the concert halls of the world.

Early coal mining in Cape Breton

STEEL TOWN

Sydney is Cape Breton's unofficial capital, the island's largest community and only city, and as different from other island towns as day is from night. For it is a steel city, and it is steel that has made not only the city but its populace a place and people apart.

In an island almost wholly populated by men and women of Scots and French descent, Sydney has a black community, the only one on the island, and thousands of people of mixed English, Irish, Welsh, Polish, Jewish, Ukrainian, Lebanese, and German blood, the descendants of immigrants who came to work in the steel mill, Cape Breton's largest industrial plant, or to operate some retail business. For generations the giant steel works in the east end dominated life in the town, later city, and its fluctuations, from busy prosperity to the austerity of recession or depression, were reflected in every aspect of the Sydney economy.

Much has changed, however, in recent years; the steel plant no longer dominates as once it did. The plant's work force has diminished with the demand for Canadian steel, and a multi-million dollar modernization program now underway, which will make the plant again competitive in world markets, will stablize the work force at a lower level than before, as technology takes over from sheer manpower. Other industries have sprung up to replace the old one-plant economy, and Sydney is a dynamic, expanding community, very much the business centre of the island.

Yet for all that, Sydney is still a steel town, the tall smokestacks the city's principal landmark, belching their orange plumes of pollution out to sea as they have done since the days when that smoke was regarded as a sign of progress and prosperity, rather than the island's shame in this environmentally conscious age.

To the visitor, Sydney offers all the bounce and vigor to be expected of a Canadian city on the make. A series of mirror-walled towers rise from its waterfront. It boasts a new convention centre, and a professional hockey team inhabits its spanking new sports arena. It is home to University College of Cape Breton and has a lovely little park, complete with ducks, set in its midst, along with plenty of pleasantly-treed streets and gracious homes, but by and large it is a lunchpail town, a working man's city, and its amenities reflect his interests. It is the communications and entrepreneurial centre of the island, with its own daily newspaper, television and radio stations. Its modern hotels and motels, its French restaurant and new high-tech industries notwithstanding, Sydney still considers itself a steel town. Just ask any Cape Bretoner!

Pouring steel at SYSCO

THE PARK

Cape Breton Highlands National Park is a sort of island within an island, a little kingdom of unspoiled wilderness inhabited mostly by wild birds and animals. Set in the northern part of Cape Breton, the park runs from east coast to west, enclosing hundreds of miles of the island's most magnificent scenery, including forest and mountain, rivers and beaches. More than any other, this is the region of Cape Breton that most visitors come to see, as it includes most of the scenic Cabot Trail and its awesome panoramas.

There is much to see and do in the park; little lakes, reached only by footpath; lovely beaches, picturesque waterfalls. There are campgrounds and picnic areas, all supervised and serviced, and there are any number of look-offs and parking areas for the benefit of photographers wishing to capture on film some of the especially spectacular views. Everything possible has been done to make the park a safe and convenient place for the casual visitor without spoiling the natural beauty of the park.

Yet this is much more than a tourist attraction. The park is a wildlife refuge, and within its boundaries are mile upon mile of forest, mountain and river, all completely untouched and unspoiled by man. This is home for much of the island's indigenous wildlife, large and small, as well as breeding grounds for a variety of animals being introduced into the island habitat. Moose, for example, have been successfully reintroduced into Cape Breton after an absence of centuries, reared under park protection before migrating to other parts of the island. Fish as well as animals can be raised here under protected circumstances, and all wildlife is left undisturbed in its natural state, rather than penned in cages or made into park pets for tourist entertainment. In this park, animals come first, humans, for all their amenities, a long way second.

Every visitor will have his or her own favorite area of the park, but nothing here is more redolent of the flavor and character of the island than The Lone Shieling. Set just off the highway high up the east coast, this is a tiny bit of Old Scotland put down in a Nova Scotia setting of idyllic beauty; a primitive shepherd's cot beside a sparkling stream and surrounded by a grove of birch and maple. Lost and lonely and breathtakingly beautiful, it is a tiny gem waiting to be discovered, hidden just off the beaten path.

Cape Breton Highlands National Park has many such treasures, and should not be visited by the tourist who is in a hurry!

Lone Shieling in autumn

TOURISM

Cottagers and casual visitors have been enjoying the beauty of Cape Breton for a long time, but it is only in the years following World War Two that the island has developed into a tourist attraction. The growing number of automobiles made Cape Breton reachable from other parts of Canada, the completion of the Trans Canada Highway from coast to coast made travelling here more comfortable and, above all, the building of a causeway across the Strait of Canso, replacing a tedious and time-consuming ferry run, marked the beginning of commercial tourism. Since the 1950s, when the culmination of these three developments began to make itself felt, the numbers of visitors to Cape Breton have grown steadily, year by year, and the facilities for their accommodation and entertainment have grown with them.

Tourism is today undoubtedly the island's single most promising new industry, and certainly the one that has grown faster than any other. Today the investment in visitor housing and catering is measured in the millions of dollars, and the island is visited annually by thousands of visitors, arriving now in charter buses from Canada and the United States, by ferry from Newfoundland, and by private automobile from every part of the continent.

The new tourist accommodations have brought benefit to Cape Bretoners as well as to the tourist. The attractive new restaurants and hotels are thronged with locals as well as visitors 'from away'; golf courses and beaches, developed for tourists have added new amenities for nearby residents, and have changed and expanded the island way of life. Dining out is now an attractive option for families living almost anywhere on the island, and a weekend at the beach is a familiar summer diversion.

But it is employment, for mature men and women as well as for young people, that the new tourist industry chiefly represents, an especially attractive development for a region traditionally limited in its range of opportunities.

Yet for all its rapid expansion, tourism on Cape Breton is remarkably unobtrusive. The island has managed to keep its charm and character and scenic beauty unmarred by commercial development, so that it is now, if possible, even more beautiful than in the days when it was known only by the discerning few. Typical of these tourist facilities which blend with their surroundings is Keltic Lodge, the flagship of the industry. Operated by the Province of Nova Scotia, the lodge sits on its own headland jutting into the sea, above a magnificent pink beach, its buildings, golf course and ski runs actually enhancing its magnificent location.

On Cape Breton, "tourism is beautiful, dear."

THE VILLAGES

In Cape Breton, most people live in or near a village. Life in the island's one city, Sydney, or towns — Glace Bay, Port Hawkesbury — is considered too confining to suit the lifestyle of most Cape Bretoners, and the island moves at the pace of the easy-going village tempo, where neckties are worn to church and funerals and a fellow is never in too much of a hurry to exchange a little friendly chat with a neighbour. Things jog along very comfortably in island villages, and the land is dotted with them.

Not only are villages thick on the ground, but they have been there for a very long time, with roots going back two centuries or more. Most of them developed around an industry, such as a fishing port or a sawmill, or perhaps because of a convenient location at a rivermouth, a bridge or ferry, a sheltered valley. They vary greatly in size, from miniature towns with a wide range of facilities, to mere hamlets clustered around a church and graveyard, for no village is complete without at least one church. But they also vary greatly in character, each with its own distinctive charm, and it is this which makes Cape Breton's villages so attractive to the visitor.

Some are scenically beautiful; Whycocomagh around its bay, perhaps, or Mabou's church spires floating above a wide river. Others have a sort of quaintness which makes them seem like stage sets; Arichat, for example, or Main-a-Dieu. Others reflect the character of the industry that made them; Inverness, the shadow of a company town, or Dingwall, the epitome of the no-nonsense fishing port. Many are redolent of the sea; Neil's Harbour or St. Peters, while others reflect the remoteness of their setting, like Capstick or Bay St. Lawrence, at the very tip of rugged Cape North.

But if the coastal communities reflect the hardness of unforgiving rock and sea, Cape Breton's inland villages are often idyllically beautiful, their neat churchyards reflecting the generations of farm families who have lived and worshipped there.

Every visitor will have his favorite island village, whether it be the Gallic simplicity of Petit Etang or the color and charm of Baddeck, but the truth is that virtually every village here has its own distinctive character, and choice depends upon the circumstances in which the visitor sees it and upon his or her individual taste.

Certainly there are few more rewarding pastimes than visiting Cape Breton's innumerable villages, and some people collect photographs or impressions of them as a philatelist collects stamps. And what collection could be complete without, say a Judique or a Portree, a Port Hood or a Mira River?

LUMBERING

Lumbering, or 'working in the woods' as it is called locally, is a way of life in Cape Breton, as it has been for generations. Just about everything is built of wood here where every man is his own carpenter, and the thick forests of spruce and birch crowd in on every side. From the earliest times lumbering has been a primary island industry, at first purely for domestic use but later devoted mostly to supply the overseas demand for both finished wood and timber logs.

But with the coming of universal education and a reading public in Britain, Europe and the United States numbered in the millions, newspaper sales soared and the resultant demand for newsprint added a new market for softwood. Cape Breton found itself in the forefront of a new and booming pulpwood industry, producing and shipping softwood logs to a seemingly insatiable market. A declining literacy and the exploitation of softwood forests in other parts of the world has stabilized the market in recent years, but pulpwood is today a major island export, and working in the woods to produce it is still a feature of island life.

In the old days, it was a matter of axe and handsaw, felling and trimming tree trunks by gangs of men usually working from their nearby homes, and hauling the logs out with chains and horses. Today, of course, the power saw and motorized equipment have made horse and handsaw obsolete, although the horse is still used in difficult hillside locations or other places where conditions make powered vehicles impractical.

Today, pulpwood harvesting is a skilled and specialized business, the trimmed logs being carried out by enormous machines called 'tree harvesters,' then loaded onto large trucks by more mechanical marvels and carried off to market. The timber trucks, with their vast burdens towering high above them, are a familiar sight along any Cape Breton highway, as are the stacks of piled pulpwood in roadside yards. Delivery is made either to the big pulpmill at Port Hawkesbury or to the pulp steamers which call regularly at coastal ports, and at Baddeck and Iona in the Bras d'Or lakes, for shipment overseas.

But with the steady development of island housing, the domestic market for finished lumber continues to grow. The little sawmills to be found on the outskirts of almost every village are being replaced by modern computerized plants capable of turning out sawn and planed lumber of every sort for the building trade, and other factories have sprung up here and there to manufacture such specialized wood products as doors and windows and panelling.

The process and the product may have changed over the years, but 'working in the woods' will always be a way of life in Cape Breton.

SHIPS AND WRECKS

From its earliest beginnings, ships have been an integral part of Cape Breton life. All the island's earliest settlers arrived by ship, since the Viking long-ships explored its coastline and the Hector brought its first shipload of Highland Scots into Pictou Harbour. Ships of every maritime nation have called at Cape Breton ports, but the island itself has built and operated seagoing vessels since the French constructed their frigates in 18th century Louisbourg, and Scottish carpenters sent their staunch little packets to the West Indies for sugar and rum.

Today its causeway to the mainland has eased Cape Breton's dependence on the sea, but no mere roadway, however convenient, can replace the infinite variety and limitless capacity of ships as carriers of the island's growing, and ever-changing, trade. Big ships steam up the Bras d'Or into the very heart of the island, to transport gypsum from the workings at Little Narrows to ports all down the eastern seaboard of the United States, as far as Texas and Louisiana. Ships with peculiar names and exotic ports of registry carry pulpwood from the island's forests of spruce to the papermills of northern Europe, and big colliers carry island coal to the power generating stations of what islanders still call 'Upper Canada.'

But new ships are arriving in Cape Breton as carriers in the island's latest, and most promising, trade; tourism. Sleek white cruise ships are now a regular feature of the Sydney waterfront, carrying thousands of camera-toting Americans all eager to enjoy and record the varied attractions of the island.

Across the harbour, North Sydney is the terminal of the giant ferries operating daily to Newfoundland, carrying not only hundreds of motorists and their cars but scores of trucks and trailers, laden with every sort of merchandise, for Cape Breton is the vital link joining Newfoundland to mainland Canada.

Inevitably, the sea has exacted its toll from all this wealth of shipping. Its rockbound coasts, its offshore rocks and islands, its strategic position athwart the main shipping routes into the Gulf of St. Lawrence and the fishing grounds of the Grand Banks, have made Cape Breton the site of innumerable shipwrecks. From Cape North to the Mira the coastline is studded with wrecks, especially at St. Paul's island to the north, Scatarie Island off the southeast tip and Isle Madam at the mouth of the Canso Strait. Rusty wrecks still project forlornly in the surf here and there, ancient cannon are revealed in the sifting sand of an island beach, riven hulls still loom dimly through the murky waters of the coastal seabed.

For the scuba diver, Cape Breton offers an abundance of wrecks to explore, especially in Louisbourg harbour where an ancient French fleet still lies beneath the frowning bastions of the great fortress.

Bluenose II sailing near Baddeck

CAPE BRETONERS

As might be expected of a region of such distinctive character, Cape Breton island has produced a host of remarkable people, their personalities shaped and sharpened by its unique environment and their talents reflecting the island way of life. Angus MacAskill, the Cape Breton giant who grew up in the Englishtown area in the early part of the 19th century, epitomized the island pioneer values; it was his enormous strength, rather than his seven-and-a-half-foot height, which made him a legend here in his own lifetime.

The veneration of education among early Scots settlers produced a great number of scholars in every branch of learning. They won their knowledge the hard way, beginning in primitive one-roomed schoolhouses, often miles from their homes; Dr. Sydney Smith, the celebrated president of the University of Toronto, was brought up on Port Hood Island, a tiny enclave off Cape Breton's northwest shore. Innumerable judges, lawyers, professors and clergymen spent their early years in island homes before attaining prominence in other parts of the world; a single family in Baddeck, the Bethunes, has produced three generations of disting-

uished medical doctors, and a nearby house was the home of Hugh MacLennan, Canada's most illustrious author.

Politics is in the Cape Breton blood, and a host of famous politicians call the island home; Nova Scotia's premier John Buchanan and Senators Alan MacEachen, Alan Graham and Lowell Murray are typical examples. In journalism, former Ottawa authority and *Macleans* editor Blair Fraser was a Cape Breton native, as was the late Nathan Cohen, perhaps the most respected of all Canadian drama critics.

Sports are a way of life in Cape Breton, and innumerable islanders have starred in the National Hockey League; Bobby Smith and Mike McPhee of the Canadiens, Alan MacInnes of the Flames, Paul Boutilier of the Islanders and Paul MacLean of the Red Wings are recent examples, while Danny Gallivan from Sydney was probably the best-known hockey broadcaster since Foster Hewitt.

But perhaps the most famous Cape Bretoner of them all is a stout, middle-aged woman from Big Pond. Rita MacNeil, in the battered fedora which has become her trademark and with her inimitable singing style, has made the island famous the world over in her endless succession of hit songs, written by herself. Sung with compelling virtuosity, her music and voice reflect, as nothing else has done, the lights and shadows of Cape Breton life.

James B. Lamb

James Lamb is a former naval officer, journalist and newspaper publisher who has written a number of books on various subjects, including the best-selling *The Corvette Navy,* and *The Hidden Heritage.* An acclaimed stylist, many reviewers have called him "a master of the language." He is a keen yachtsman, and lives with his wife in a house overlooking the Great Bras d'Or at Big Harbour, near Baddeck, N.S.

Warren Gordon

Warren Gordon operates Gordon Photographic Limited, a major photographic studio and scenic gallery in downtown Sydney, Cape Breton. He has received regional and national recognition for his work, including the degree of Craftsman of Photographic Arts. In pursuit of new and unique images he has undertaken photographic expeditions to Hong Kong, China, the Caribbean and the Canadian Rocky Mountains.